Church
Meetings
that
Work

---

gaylord noyce

an alban institute publication

Library of Congress Catalog Card Number 94-78332
ISBN 1-56699-132-3

CONTENTS

CHAPTER 1

Why Meet?

Jane Swiggin glowered at Jerry and pouted, "Another church meeting! I love St. John's, but how I hate those interminable meetings. You know my oxymoron for the week? 'Important church meeting.' That's almost always what the notice says. But it's a contradiction in terms. They should admit it in the announcement: 'Time-wasting and unimportant!'"

Jerry, a patient husband for fifteen good years, tried to explain once more: "How else are you going to run a church or any organization? Bill Schlaughter would be a tyrant of a pastor if we didn't have committee meetings. How would he know what people were really thinking? Where would ideas come from except from his own head? How would we keep in touch with each other now that we have almost four hundred members? We have just as many meetings at my office. Sometimes I think we don't really produce anything all day—we just push a few papers between meetings. I'll admit, however, that you and I are different. You don't like groups the way I do. I kind of enjoy watching the whole process move along."

Meetings are everywhere. Most organizations could do with fewer, but some need more. Meetings serve many purposes, not all of them obvious. Some meetings are for planning, for keeping people informed, or for encouraging people who are discouraged. Some are for making decisions or for easing quarrels. Some are for helping alcoholics and other addicts. Some are for negotiating international arms reductions and trade relations. Society almost lives by meetings. No less, the church.

The good news is this: Unavoidable as they are, meetings need not be dull, destructive, or even unduly time-consuming. The purpose of this book is to help you lead or coach or take part in church meetings that work.

Jane and Jerry may think meetings are a modern phenomenon born of a fast-paced, complex society. But meetings have probably been around since our first progenitors held a necessary family conference. Adam triggered it by asking, "What shall we do about Cain?"

An Early Church Meeting

We can read of an early church meeting in Acts 15. This report reveals some of the reasons for meetings and some of the elements that make meetings effective.

Paul and Barnabas return to Antioch after their eventful first missionary journey. The gospel message had attracted Gentiles into the budding Jewish groups of Jesus' followers. Paul and Barnabas had welcomed them.

However, we read, "Certain individuals came down from Judea and were teaching..., 'Unless you [follow] the custom of Moses, you cannot be saved.'" Paul and Barnabas disagree, and there is "no small dissension." Which way will the new movement go? Paul leads a delegation, which makes the long trip through Phoenicia and Samaria all the way to Jerusalem. There the issues are joined again. Paul's group meets the opposition face-to-face. Some new Christians "who belonged to the sect of the Pharisees" say, "It is necessary for [the Gentile converts] to be circumcised."

No organization or movement can be free of new circumstances or changing opinions that necessitate response. Excluding the possibility of a single autocrat who has absolute power and unlimited time and competence, that response requires negotiation, a meeting.

In Acts 15, a meeting of the proper authorities (apostles and elders) is convened in the proper place—Jerusalem. Participants are certified ("Paul and Barnabas and some of the others were appointed" to attend). In the ensuing discussions, participants cite the grounds of their opinions (Peter: "In the early days, God made a choice among you, that I should [reach out to] the Gentiles"). They refer to their own observations ("God testified to them by giving them the Holy Spirit"). They use logic ("Why are you putting God to the test?"). They cite ancient sources ("This agrees with the words of the prophets"). They hear a proposal for compromise and settlement (James: "I have reached the decision that we should not trouble those Gentiles who are turning to God"). The assembly concurs ("with the consent of the whole church"), and the participants publicize their decision, sending some from their own number back to Antioch with Paul and Barnabas.

Good Precedents

We could wish that all church councils would do as well. Note the five points just reviewed from Acts.

1. The meeting took up a new proposal rather than squelched it prematurely. Although some probably did, others were there who did not say, "We've never done it that way before."

2. The group considered alternative points of view; apparently no one was bullied.

3. The conference used firsthand accounts rather than hearsay and prejudice. Paul and Barnabas "told of all the signs and wonders that God had done through them among the Gentiles."

4. Godly faith, not mere political advantage, defined and motivated their deliberations.

5. When a clear decision was reached ("to abstain only from things polluted by idols and from fornication and from whatever has been strangled and from blood"), it was intentionally publicized. No one is reported to have said, "You never told us," or "I don't read the church newsletter that often."

Given all these substantial reasons for meetings, why do meetings go sour? Why does Jane find them boring, inconsequential, and frustrating? It is mainly because people haven't thought critically about meetings.

Most of us can enjoy meetings far more than we do and make them more worthwhile as well. We can learn how meetings work, and on that basis, as leaders and members alike, we can run better meetings.

Thinking about Meetings

Church meetings serve more ends than we often know.

Obviously, we need to make decisions—about the church budget, about new leadership when a pastor resigns and leaves, about the local chapter of Labrador retriever breeders using the children's chapel during a statewide convention. Planning and decision-making meetings are our chief concern in this book.

Second, meetings are for learning. Sometimes a meeting is comparable to a good seminar or classroom session. Learning can facilitate better planning and decision making. We share new information and develop new combinations of old learning in a face-to-face process that promotes insight and growth.

There is a third and often unnoticed purpose for meetings, however, even decision-making meetings. Ignored, the need for it can disrupt meetings so seriously that Jane Swiggin and her ilk may give up on participation altogether. Meetings express and nurture our social nature.

Humans are social animals. We are created for each other in community. Meetings are actually a primary way we of the modern world rub shoulders and maintain human touch. Jane may come to a meeting intent on discussing the all-church mission increase, on voting a yes or a no on it, and then getting away to watch a favorite TV show or to check on a teen-ager's math assignment or to prepare the morrow's presentation at her job. But if the meeting proper is brittle and inhospitable or, on the other hand, is cluttered and prolonged with seemingly irrelevant banter, Jane can despair.

We will discuss this more as we go on, but at this stage two points are obvious. First, if she understands their social dimension, Jane will be a little more patient with some small talk in meetings. And second, the stronger chairperson will realize the advantages of separating the meeting's business time from most of its social time. Then when she is pressed for time, Jane can leave early, skipping the social period after business, and even come late if there is usually a time of introductory chatter.

This hidden function (and benefit) of most meetings deserves attention as much as efficiency does. Through both business and social exchanges in meetings we strengthen the web of human relations. We make our lives more human.

The social weight that meetings bear varies, of course, with the subculture. A business-oriented WASPy suburb may devote little time to weeknight socializing. People from a rural community may linger long, telling old tales, inventing new ones, and passing along the communal news. A Hispanic or African-American congregation may mix socializing and decision making together without anyone feeling fretful in Jane's way at all.

Most church meetings run two hours but could be just as useful in an hour and a half. Meetings that move along energetically are better attended. Separating most of the social chitchat from the committee's designated work will help shorten meetings in itself. Jane will be pleased. Conveners and chairpeople who prepare their agendas carefully and who understand leading can strengthen a congregation's life immeasurably.

Jerry Swiggin told Jane that he enjoyed meetings. Jerry was blessed by a relaxed curiosity that helped him sit loose to the time slippage in a meeting. He could toy playfully with ideas about hidden agendas, cultural differences, and group process, and at the same time he could participate seriously in a collective effort of creativity and planning. Jerry enjoyed people not only one by one but also in clusters. He will be a help as we move along. So will Jane. A good committee will learn to satisfy both Jane and Jerry, different as they are from each other.

CHAPTER 2

The Chairperson's Job

Jane Swiggin's friend Rebecca Withers had been chosen to chair the Consistory, St. John's fourteen-member governing and coordinating body, a group elected by the whole congregation at its annual meeting. Rebecca came to Jane with a question, "You've been unhappy with a lot of our church meetings, I hear. How can I improve the meetings I'll be leading this year?"

Jane was quick to reply, "Help your group stick to business." Then she added, to illustrate, "I'm on the Education Commission. Henry Jacobs, our present chairman, never seems to want to interrupt the flow of a conversation that is drifting off track."

It is the chairperson's task to lead a committee, to help it "tend to business." This does not mean making decisions for the committee. Otherwise, meetings would serve only as information sharing or social gatherings. Nor does it mean rejecting the notion that meetings have a social function and can benefit from humor and lightheartedness. It does mean that the leader shoulders several vital responsibilities.

Good Leadership

Jane might continue by naming the following five functions of good leaders:

1. Articulate the vision.

2. Tend to external relationships.

3. Foster communication and deliberation.

4. Provide guidance for decision making.

5. Monitor follow-through between meetings.

Articulating the Vision

We humans are creatures of purpose. We are the dreamers among the
animals. A committee or a congregation— or a nation, for that matter—
needs a sense of direction. The mission of a group is not always clearly
understood. It can be assumed or felt mainly "in the bones," but the
leader must also give it words.

A committee cannot long function like the airline pilot who is said
to have announced, "The bad news is, we're lost! The good news is,
we're making very good time."

Defining the mission of a group merits careful attention by a leader. If a team of managers defines its goal as selling typewriters, their
business shrinks when typewriters turn obsolete. If those managers see
their task as selling word-processing equipment, they can easily shift to
include electronic computers, printers, and photocopiers in their product
line. Their business will do better in event of change.

A church Education Committee may see its goal as managing a
Sunday School for children or it may take a broader view which per-
ceives that the whole parish is a learning community. In the latter case
adult education comes naturally into the committee's purview, and the
group will also work with parents and the persons responsible for worship, fellowship activities, and mission giving.

The leader can express the goals of a group in various ways.
Creeds and calls to worship help the congregation do that in weekly worship. At memorial services a minister will often begin, "We are gathered
together to hear the word of Scripture for our comfort and to give thanks
to God for the life of Charles Swenson"—or whomever. Weddings have
a similar opening: "To unite this man and this woman in holy matri-
mony." A chairperson often begins a meeting, "Our purpose as a committee is such and such," or "Our meeting tonight is for the following
purposes." Then he or she circulates an agenda or helps the group build

one with a brief discussion. In either case, the framework helps the committee tend to its business and exclude extraneous, distracting moves.

Vision ought to come naturally to church meetings, but it doesn't. Our personalities do not shed their clothing of self-interest and scrappiness simply because of a prayer at meeting's start and meeting's end. The group's decision-making process is similar enough to that of competitive, political encounters elsewhere in our lives that we assume and exhibit self-aggrandizing goals for the church. The church through us forgets its call to service and faithful witness, and it ends up measuring itself by the numbers—balance on hand, the count of the pews. We need chairpeople who can help us approach church meetings with the same contrition and openness to the Spirit's leading as are appropriate in worship. This the leader can do and thoughtful members can do by sharing their vision for Christ's church in the world.

Tending to External Relationships

The vision articulated by the leader of a group relates to a context. If the CEO of the team selling word processors, she or he keeps an eye on the technology of information flow, printing styles, the foreign and domestic competition, academic, business, and personal needs and habits. Although their knowledgeability is all to the good, subordinates in the business do not have that same responsibility. The leader may, of course, delegate part of this assignment.

A church committee chairperson needs to keep in touch with other events and plans in the congregation's life and effectively describe to the committee that wider setting and its implications for the committee's work. For example, Henry Jacobs, whom Jane criticized, needs to advocate for education at St. John's but also to inform his committee what is going on in the wider church. For this purpose among others, he is probably a member of the church's governing council. He may choose to delegate his responsibility, of course, asking Jane to go to Consistory or Council in his place from time to time. If he does, however, he will need to brief Jane in advance and debrief her afterward. Either way, the wider context of the group's work is brought in by the leader's initiative.

The leader will understand more than most people the structural context of the group. This context sets the balance of the committee's freedom to act and the limits to its action. "Going through channels," we call it. Constitutions and sets of bylaws do not always spell out clearly these options and limits. The chairperson's job requires an ability to identify with a larger organization beyond one's own responsibility. The Social Outreach Commission at St. John's may claim the freedom to write the local newspaper editor in its own name, not implying that the whole congregation stands behind it, but it should nonetheless, as in most congregations, inform the Consistory and Bill Schlaughter. Its action, no matter how clearly it spells out the modesty of its claim—"speaking only for ourselves"—implicates to some extent the whole congregation. The congregation is blessed that offers trust and freedom of initiative to all its committees, committees that have self-starting leaders who understand the need for channels, for mutual information sharing, and for a cooperative spirit.

Fostering Communication and Deliberation

This third assignment of a leader moves into the brass tacks area of making meetings work. Sharing information and ideas makes good decisions possible. We will find various ways of enhancing this process as we proceed. Gathering information goes only part way, however. A meeting of minds for good decisions involves discussing options, putting alternatives next to each other to see if a third possibility, better than either, emerges. It involves looking over one's shoulder at the interests and concerns of others not present. It involves making sure that the group as a whole is committed to a decision in more than vote only.

Deliberative process opens the way for conversational meandering and social chitchat that can sabotage a meeting. The chairperson should function a little like an old farm cream separator, siphoning off the lighter elements till the social hour when necessary. The chairperson firmly but tactfully interrupts, setting a standard, building a committee ethos: "Good story, Mike. But I think we need to get back to the agenda."

Fostering deliberative process is a skill that will claim an entire chapter (chapter 4) as we proceed. It is the heart of most committee work.

Providing Guidance for Decision Making

The executive function is most impressive, of course, when in a large assembly a leader calls for a vote, announces "the ayes have it" and instructs a clerk to mark it down. Similar moments occur with consensus building in groups as small as pairs or triads. Chapter 5 describes various patterns of decision making. In a small church group, the formal executive manner is inappropriate and may be counter-productive. Nonetheless, the leader nails down the decision with some precision. "It is agreed then, that Stenson can go ahead with the roofing contract." "We have now decided on the Victorian Lace dinnerware for the parlor."

Monitoring Follow-Through between Meetings

The chairperson monitors overall progress on commitments planned at meetings. "Mike, will you call Bess about the date? If there is any question, call me right away." "Janice, can you meet with Ken on the arrangements for the kitchen?" "John, will you pass on the suggestion to Bill Schlaughter about the service?"

If the leader is uneasy about any of these assignments, he or she will need to do some quiet checking after about a week, making sure these commitments have been or are being honored. Tact is important, and a basic trust of committee members, but this monitoring ranks high among the chairperson's responsibilities.

A Few Caveats

After this brief focus on the chairperson's role, we need to step back with some warnings. We of today's church know something about the faults of hierarchy, whether it be in government, business, education, or religion. Hierarchy can rob people of their creativity and leave the church deprived. It can oppress people, demean and exploit them. In short, efficient as it appears in the short run, it is ultimately counterproductive.

The chairperson is thus not fundamentally a giver of orders. He or she facilitates a process—the process of responding to change, the process of generating new ideas, the process of generating new thought, the process of solving problems, the process of guiding and coordinating human enterprise.

The thoughtful chairperson therefore strikes a balance between assertive guidance and a more passive stance that allows the group to move ahead on its own, as it were. I can illustrate by describing one leader who is too imperious and one who is too passive.

Simon Fielding is too imperious, too authoritarian. He chairs the Education Board of a sister congregation, not far from St. John's. Simon believes that his ideas, which are good, should claim plenty of respect, and he is right. However, he is an impatient man, eager for his church to mount a more effective adult education program. He proposes to the Board a new schedule of adult teaching sessions; he lines up speakers from outside the congregation and tells Board members what functions they should assume—two for refreshments, two others for publicity, one to meet and host each guest.

The program does not go well. One member gets publicity in late. Another never follows up as host. The social hour is meager and graceless. Attendance wanes after the first two sessions. When pastor Art Everton tries to find the flaws, he has little choice but to conclude it is Simon's style. Simon doesn't work *with* people; he bosses them. He doesn't listen openly for other ideas since he knows his own are plenty good. Simon doesn't wait for his Board members' enthusiasm to develop. Therefore, the members don't claim Simon's new program as their own. They don't invest themselves in it.

At the opposite extreme, in a campus-based ministry affiliated with St. John's, Anna Fortier, a seminary intern, has gathered a team of students and faculty to plan a week of emphasis on the liberation of women. She wants to be a facilitator. "Everyone is equally important," she tells the group. "We'll not have a chairperson." After three months, six two-hour meetings total, nothing has taken shape at all. She tells her professor/supervisor that she has been meticulous in avoiding hierarchy. Since every member could make her contribution, an effective community should have emerged. After discussion with her mentor Anna realizes as never before that leadership requires a more active role in coordination than she has been offering.

Democratic leadership does not mean either hierarchy or tyranny, but neither does it mean there's no need for someone to help a group pull its diversity toward consensus.

Proper Assertive Leadership

The need for assertiveness from the chair varies widely according to the size of a meeting, its experience together, and its general cohesiveness. A committee of four barely needs a chair; a congregational meeting of seventy-five needs careful agenda planning and a formal set of rules (usually *Robert's Rules of Order*) to channel its deliberative process.

Most groups will profit from coaching about better meetings. This can be done easily enough through conscious attention to prcess during regular meetings. Chapter 8 describes a plausible day-long training event.

The chairperson in a group has the assignment to step back and assess morale and effectiveness over and over. Minor changes may be initiated for improvement. The meeting time, the location, and/or the communication system may be shifted. Meeting in homes instead of at the church may help or hinder. Using chairs instead of overstuffed furniture, sitting in circles instead of formal rows, adding chalkboards and newsprint for recording information—all such considerations are part of an alert chairing competence.

Agenda is as important as any other major responsibility. Having an agenda posted in clear print or photocopied and circulated accomplishes several things. It organizes priorities. It organizes time. It tells Jane and Mike and the others whether they can add a comment that is relatively unimportant because there seems to be time for it, or whether to hold their tongues because there is so much still to come. It helps a recording secretary follow the meeting and write it up.

The good leader will be sensitive to more subtle influences as well. Jane Swiggin, for example, wants the pace of a meeting speeded up. Rapid dialogue in even old movie classics often proceeds with a noticeable split-second interval of silence between the actors' speeches. In contemporary films, the gap is closed. If a leader recognizes in some members a tendency to run on repetitiously or to run down slowly at the end of comments, a gentle (sometimes firm!) interruption that passes the conversational ball to someone else is often welcome and effective. "Yes, that's useful," the leader says quickly when even the fast-talking rambler has to catch a breath, "I would like Bess to tell us her experience of that disagreement..." or whatever. At other times, if a point is well made, a silence that lets the point sink in may be equally important.

Leadership Is a Function, Not a Person

One more perspective on leadership is helpful: Leadership is a function not limited to a designated chairperson. The designated leader may in fact sit back and let leadership bounce around the room during a meeting. The presenter of a report can field questions that arise, without intervention from the chair. "Mike, let's have your subcommittee report now; you can manage the discussion of it yourself." The leader is thinking to himself or herself at such a time, *Mike is both fair-minded and knowledgeable about this. He can chair this. I need only keep an eye on the clock and keep the agenda on schedule. I don't need to intrude at all unless discussion lags.*

An advocate for a position may engage in exchanges with two or three others, again without direct management from the leader. The chairperson will step in only if arguments get personal or hostile or off the track. If a meeting is in the home of the chairperson and the telephone rings, the discussion should usually continue even if the presider has to step out briefly. For large, formal meetings, Robert's rules require the chairperson, if keen on entering debate, to step aside, temporarily handing over guidance to someone else.

Leadership is a function, not a person. Remembering that, a chairperson can remain a facilitator of effective consensus and creative group action. The leader doesn't take center stage. The work of Christ does. Moreover, much of the controversy to which we now turn will not arise.

CHAPTER 3

When Troubles Brew

Most disagreements in church meetings can be turned to good account. Disagreements generate emotional interest. A seasoned chairperson, therefore, like an expert in martial arts, moves with that energy and guides it toward constructive purpose.

We should, therefore, resist our usual reflex in the face of controversy—that of avoidance. The initial question should be, "Is this a healthy controversy brewing?" rather than, "How can we avoid this?" Granted, that kind of response is not easy to come by, but healthy conflict can clear the air and mobilize creativity. Avoidance makes for more meaningless meetings when people say, "Nothing happened." Unhealthy, or mismanaged, of course, a conflict may well be destructive.

An illustration: A southern church I served still owes much of its identity as a truly faithful fellowship and a force for its city's good to a controversy that shook it to the roots fifty years ago, well before my time there. The storm shrank its membership by about a third, but a decade later most members said the event had been providential.

In the 1940s, when the lines of segregation in Raleigh, North Carolina, were still rigid, United Church, a white congregation, invited Ralph Bunche to address its well-attended midwinter Institute of Religion. Bunche, who was then trusteeship division director for the United Nations Secretariat and was later awarded Nobel Peace prize for his mid-East diplomacy, held the highest UN office ever held by an American and was an African-American. That he should address a southern audience, after an integrated dinner, and in the civic auditorium, was, in the culture of that time and place, unprecedented and inflammatory. The pro-Bunche forces prevailed in United Church's controversy, and the minority left the congregation. The Church, although seemingly decimated, survived and found itself blessed with a profound sense of its calling and purpose. The controversy could probably not have been avoided with anything resembling religious integrity.

The Imbalance that Moves Us Forward

Like the laws of nature, the laws of meetings mean nothing happens without disequilibrium, some pressure from one side or another. The pressure throws the organism off a static dead center. It redirects momentum and energy.

Human life always involves disequilibrium—temperature differentials, muscle tensions, breathing and hunger, sexual drive, boredom, curiosity, imagination. Stress is a fact of life. It is a pressure to change style, to shift course, to move forward. Total immobility or stability is only a fact of death. Pressure may come from new ideas, from a change in the environment, from a cultural shift fostered by the media, or from a changed economy. In a church the pressure may issue from a layperson's creativity, from a denominational resolution, from the local pastor. It may be a personality feud, the freezing to death of a homeless man under a bridge, the enthusiasm of a teen-ager back from a Third World service project, an added tenor for the choir. Something needs tending because a reliable leader has moved away. The windows need cleaning, the belfry painting. The church year brings Advent again. A leader dies. The neighborhood shifts its religious makeup.

Once we accept disequilibrium as a potential gift of the Spirit, as one dimension of the way all social organisms function, we are less prone to back away from every occasion of stress. We should be more concerned about a lack of any tension at all.

In St. John's Consistory, disequilibrium can arise from a new concern expressed in one of Bill Schlaughter's sermons, or an idea from Henry or his Education Commission or from any one of the church's four hundred members. It may be a discovery of termites in a corner of the parish house, a demographic change in the community, the departure of a church "pillar," a town school board proposal about a baccalaureate program, the need for better lighting in the kitchen.

Trouble is brewing when differences of opinion gather emotional, factional steam. Conflict is more than a difference of opinion. It is a difference in which people's emotions are invested. Conflict involves different loyalties, different fundamental perceptions of the world ("assumptive worlds," they have been called), and different theologies. Therefore, if we can but remember these deeper dimensions, church meetings are full of possibilities for spiritual insight.

Again, an illustration: At St. John's, most older people remember a time during the sixties when the congregation was deeply divided. Should the church engage the youth director for a second contracted year? He had led the teen-agers and a related college group on what some considered a very creative track of civil rights involvement and peace advocacy. Others saw his work as next to unpatriotic, unchristian, and slightly immoral in its militancy of method. St. John's Consistory called a congregational meeting for an airing of views. During the meeting, church members were increasingly hostile; they began to throw verbal brickbats at each other across the large sanctuary. One wise elder, however, stood up, walked deliberately to the chancel, and spoke quietly. His words not only calmed the assembly immediately. They chastened the more vitriolic debaters, and they profoundly deepened the spiritual awareness of the congregation. At that moment, the people caught a new glimpse of the body of Christ in their midst. All he said was this: "Dear friends, we are a congregation made of up of very different people. Some of us are conservative; some of us are liberal. We have a conflict on our hands, and by God's grace we're strong enough to deal with it." He made no proposals. He simply made an observation.

Tempting as it may be, avoidance builds up repressed resentments that make later disagreements more painful. It deprives the community of the healing we know in forgiveness and reconciliation, so profound a part of Christian life. It trivializes the church by tiptoeing around the important issues of our times. And it runs away from central realities of life in the body of Christ.

Dealing with Conflict

As illustrated at St. John's, when a meeting erupts in controversy, the most effective first step, which turns out often in and of itself to be a major part of healing, is the simple recognition of the conflict. This attacks the dangers of avoidance head-on.

We have the same experience in interpersonal relations: "George, I think you and I disagree on this." Based on that premise, the discussion that follows is likely to be both more comfortable and more enlightening.

Put another way, one of our goals is to transform conflict into disagreement. We try to temper an emotional and possibly irrational conflict with elements of rational insight. We do not pretend; we recognize that emotion is inevitably an element. Were it not, there would be little problem. But as the importance of acknowledgment shows, we can make better headway at first by a focus more on process than on substance. Holding the substantial questions back momentarily, we may chart a course for resolution. We might, for example, decide to seek a third party opinion, to seek more facts, to agree upon binding arbitration, or to set a date for the final vote and for meetings in the meantime.[1]

How do we apply all this as we lead a meeting? If the arguments get dangerously heated, or if they bog down, we back up: "Apparently we won't get far in carrying on the discussion just now. Let's talk about *how* we can resolve the issue. Would more information help? Shall we give the problem to someone else?" And so on.

Here is a plausible list of other steps.

1. Start with agreements.

Find what rational accord already exists. *(a)* "We have a disagreement." "Yes, I agree." *(b)* "The budget can afford a youth director?" "Yes, on that we agree, also." *(c)* "Chet has good rapport with our teens, and the youth membership has grown." *(d)* "Yes, and these are confusing times for kids." *(e)* "Yes, and we don't want them to hide out or give up; we want them to relate to the issues of our time." *(f)* "Chet has made some mistakes, but he's growing." And so on.

2. Define the issues carefully, dispassionately.

Explore descriptively just how the factions differ. This includes a description of feelings. *(a)* "We disapprove of civil disobedience that deprives others of the right to speak, even if their position appears to oppose civil rights." *(b)* "We don't think we can legislate morality, so we don't think Mrs. Holmes should be forced by law to rent out her upstairs room to people she doesn't like." *(c)* "We don't think young men should be allowed to choose for themselves which wars are okay and which are not." *(d)* "Chet has proposed all these things to our kids. Other things he's done we approve, but we feel that he has often shot from the hip."

Such assertions, patiently heard and understood, can clarify a church fight. Even more than having their own way in disputes, people want to have a voice in the decision making. And that reflective participation, of course, is of the essence of moral, communal life.

Someone defined the *church* as a "community of moral discourse." Leaders of meetings need to know that the "right" decision can be one that goes against their private convictions about what would be best. Otherwise they can become immoral moral tyrants, undercutting the work of moral thought that others must do.

3. Remember the gift of time.

Time usually tempers strong emotions. The faculty of a small school was notorious for resistance to change. However, one astute professor said there was little problem if innovators were wise. Reflecting on the monthly faculty meetings, he observed, "Nothing new will ever pass when it is simply introduced for a vote. Nevertheless, if introduced as a mere proposal at one meeting and then put to a vote a month later, it almost always passes."

Time does heal. It allows emotions to cool. One congregation faced a major controversy when several members began campaigning for the resignation of its pastor. Emotions ran high over the issue of leadership in the church by a gifted man of homosexual orientation. Emotionally charged, the fight could doubtless have been a destructive, divisive experience. The Council persuaded the pastor's opposition to participate in a learning and peacemaking process for three months while the congregation thought through (once more) its previous commitment to be "open and affirming" in relation to membership without discrimination. The final vote was 75 percent in favor of openness, and the pastor stayed on in a now-stronger church. Instead of splitting about fifty-fifty and rejecting its leadership, the congregation lost only a few (relatively inactive) members and grew in strength.

Time helps. When a discussion is bogged down and time is available, a chairperson can easily say, "We'll invest fifteen more minutes, and then I suggest we either vote or table the matter until we have more facts." Or this: "If you're willing, we can report a divided committee and ask the Vestry itself to make the decision later." On a minor matter, if emotion has largely subsided and time has run out, it is also legitimate to say, "I propose since there is no more time that we have Jane and George talk with each other and work out a compromise."

4. Seek a win-win solution.

Our competitive nature and part of our experience make us assume all too often that when anyone wins, someone else loses. We think the world always presents what we call a zero-sum opportunity only; the win-lose option and nothing else. Actually, just as often, negotiation allows a net advantage for both parties. A free marketplace, for example, makes that latter assumption: I gain money from you while you are pleased to receive my painting. We are both ahead. An emotional rejection of each other can make us ignore areas of potential agreement, but shared clarity about our several wants and needs may disclose an overlap of agreements larger than we had first believed possible. With a little creative thinking we may then strike a win-win agreement. We may invent a new solution to a problem, one from which we both gain most of what we wanted. This is the work of diplomats, mediators, and matchmakers. It is also the work of skilled chairpeople.

Personality Types and Meeting Snags

Just as the forthright recognition of controversy makes for peace, so the recognition of different personal styles can help us immeasurably in leading meetings that work.

Eavesdrop for a few minutes at a Women's Service Club (WSC) executive committee meeting at St. John's Community Parish. Sally Gordon is chairing. It is getting late. Sally has to pick up her teen-ager from an evening play rehearsal. Planning for the bazaar and for the workshop on feminism and Christian life is complete. Next year's programming is as far along as it can be pending more replies from invited guests. Fully expecting none, Sally asks if there is new business to be dealt with. She is impatient to get the meeting over.

But Donna Roper raises her hand. "I want to propose that we investigate the possibilities of a memorial garden for that area between our two buildings. A church my husband and I visited recently in Ohio has this burial area for the ashes of its members who die. It was started just ten years ago, and already it has a lot of meaning for people. And it makes more sense than the expenses of a cemetery."

Sally is nonplussed and terribly upset. She knows it's not mainly a matter of time because she will have the proposal referred to a subgroup right away. Fundamentally, she disapproves Donna's lack of orderliness. This kind of proposal should not come up out of the blue. It should have been on the agenda. Sally likes to have her meetings go according to plan. Donna, on the other hand, is an enthusiast—energetic, laughing, ready-or-not-here-I-come. She likes interruptions, unexpected changes, intuitive, less rational processes. To Sally, interruptions and intuition spell chaos.

Since ancient times we have recognized and classified different personality types. Hippocrates wrote of four temperaments—sanguine, choleric, phlegmatic, or melancholic. The Chinese speak of Yin and Yang in personality makeup. Astrologers evidently believe that birth dates and star patterns are determinants of the character we have ("I am a Cancer; you are Aquarius"), but even their perspective makes the same point— that real differences among us need recognition if we are to get along well with others. One current self-discovery tool, the Enneagram, uncovers nine personality types.

Presently, a great deal is written about personality differences between men and women. Some argue it is by nature that we differ so; others say that for better and worse, it is our nurture. Some argue the differences are good; some, insidious. Either way, the popularity of books like those by Carol Gilligan *(In a Different Voice)* [2] and Deborah Tannen *(You Just Don't Understand)* [3] show that a rehearsal of these differences strikes home. Differences of style between men and women also divide our meetings.

In sum, these perspectives underscore the fact that people do function differently. They have different styles. Committee leaders need to know this. Failure to recognize differences—and to praise God for

them—leads to trouble. If Sally could resign herself to the fact that
Donna has a different makeup, let alone bless God for it since it so nice-
ly complements her own competence as an organizer, she would spare
herself some grief and be an even better leader.

The Myers-Briggs Classification

As to personal style, the most popular classification system at present,
one that is based on the work of Carl Jung, uses a derivative instrument
called the Myers-Briggs Type Indicator. The MBTI is a simple (150-
question) personality test that charts people's self-assessed preferences
and personal styles along four axes. Through scoring our answers to
forced-choice questions, we rate ourselves, for example, as being more
extroverted (E) or introverted (I). One is more intuitive (N) or more
interested in practical sense-oriented (S) knowledge. Another axis is the
tendency to prefer thinking (T) over feeling (F) or vice versa. A final
and more subtle tension, badly named to my mind, is between judging (J)
and perceiving (P). (The judging or J-type wants things buttoned up, like
Sally. The perceiving or P-type likes things more spontaneous and unexpected, less planned out. Donna would be a P on this axis.)

All told, given the four different sets of choice (E or I, S or N, T or
F, and J or P), the MBTI recognizes sixteen personality types. A person
knowledgeable in MBTI jargon may say, for example, "I am an ENTJ; as
I see you, you must be an INFP."

Clearly, many troubles that brew at church meetings result more
from personality differences than from different ultimate loyalties or
even different ideas. An ultimate loyalty to Christ bonds us together
despite our different ways of applying that loyalty to our use of Scripture, our different life experiences and social locations that profoundly
affect our opinions, and our different gifts of mind and heart. But personality style affects meetings just as much as any of these. It expedites
meetings when people accept and enjoy the facts of difference rather
than bemoan them.[4]

The energy in conflict can more often be turned to good purpose
than not. Although the language may vary, our resources include common commitments that can be evoked—a faithful witness, loyalty to
Christ, dedication to the church. Good leaders accept the normalcy of

change and openly acknowledge tension and personality differences. The win-win goal overrides competitive win-lose ambitions. Given these resources, even when trouble brews, meetings thrive.

NOTES

1. One of the most useful of the many books on conflict management is *Getting to Yes* by Roger Fisher and William Ury (Boston: Houghton Mifflin, 1981).

2. (Cambridge, Mass.: Harvard University Press, 1982).

3. (New York: William Morrow, 1990).

4. A helpful source book for understanding the MBTI is *Please Understand Me: Character and Temperament Types* by David Kiersey and Marilyn Bates (Del Mar, Calif.: Prometheus Nemesis, 1978).

CHAPTER 4

Drawing People In

Rebecca Withers found her earlier discussion with Jane so helpful that she followed up on it. She caught Jane for a review after her first meeting chairing the board. Jane had attended in Henry's place, representing Education. "Did we do it to your satisfaction?" Rebecca asked. "Wouldn't you call that a useful meeting?"

"Not bad for starters," Jane quipped. "I liked the way you separated business from socializing, so we ended more promptly. Dave Bruckman could get home to his sick boy. It meant the rest of us could gossip over coffee a little, without feeling guilty. And Veronica, while she's dedicated enough and faithful, never likes to waste time, so she could leave instead of doing small talk, too. And I was amazed that you let those two men in the corner argue the way they did instead of interrupting them to make the meeting more peaceful."

"Now I want to get more people in on the discussion," said Rebecca. "The old guard has tended to dominate—out of good intentions, of course. But there are a lot of younger people who ought to have a voice, too."

Rebecca then asked Jane how to draw more people in on the meeting's substance. "You know, out in the parking lot after the meeting, I heard Mike Simpson and Priscilla Goldman—their cars were next to each other—talking about the new youth ministry ideas built around service projects. They should have talked in meeting. Mike and Pris have good suggestions—only we haven't drawn them in on the process at all. They are so quiet in our meetings." Jane realized that she had been quiet and, by her passivity, had probably contributed to the "boredom" of meetings where she had been present. "It isn't all the leader's fault, Rebecca, but there must be ways we can draw people in."

A truck driver, with formal education through only tenth grade, was once asked to serve on a committee for supervising a seminary student in the trucker's parish. He declined at first, saying that with his limited learning he had nothing to offer a graduate student from a major academic institution. "You don't appreciate your own importance," the pastor told him. "You know some things that no one else in the entire world knows, and they are important to Benson, our student, to hear about—how he comes across to you. He needs to know that."

The Lord's table is necessarily open not only to extroverts and leaders in the congregation but to every last soul. Let it be so also in our church meetings. Ideally, every member of a committee makes a positive contribution by speaking up. Each person, while unique, represents the thought of other similar persons, too. The total life experience in a committee of five people, if it is all accessible, adds up to an immense amount of wisdom.

The trick, of course, is helping shy ones speak up and helping others allow them space. A good friend, skilled in educational method, once made a request of her students in a fifty-member class: "Raise your hands when I name the size of a group in which you feel comfortable speaking up." She began with "fifty" and then said "forty-five" and "forty." Gradually, hands went up, but not every last one until she reached "three"!

Getting Members to Participate

Achieving participation by everyone in sizable committees takes skill.

An Open Style

Style, of course, is fundamental. The dictator doesn't genuinely seek others' opinions. The chairperson must sincerely want input and participation.

Participatory Agenda Building

The group should participate in agenda building. A last-minute call for new business is inadequate. Making the invitation one of the first steps at a meeting is far better: "You see the agenda. Are there other items we should be taking up?" Without this kind of opportunity, Jane may be half right when she says, "They never really address my concerns at those meetings."

Gatekeeping

In a classroom, the teacher can call on quiet ones. We may, with tact, do almost the same in committees. When gestures, frowns, bright eyes, or even conversations outside the meeting give us clues, we can easily offer people an opening. "Cassius, you look like you have some feeling on that; tell us what you think," or "Jane, over coffee last Sunday you said something to me about this. I wish you would share it with the whole group." One of the purposes in having someone other than the presider take notes, even in very small meetings, is to free the chair for maximum eye contact and observation. Gatekeeping ranks high among chairing skills in the informal meeting.

Buzz Groups

In boards and committees of fifteen and more, subgrouping is often essential for healthy participation. It needn't be a long interruption: "As chair, I'm going to suggest that we talk with each other for just five minutes in groups of three or four right here where we are. I want you to speculate about the reasons we didn't make our financial goal in the stewardship drive. Then we'll have a three-sentence report from each group as I list our thoughts on the board." Make the task clear. Stick to the rules and the promise about feedback. The level of involvement in these larger groups will increase noticeably.

There are other ways to get everyone's input. A self-confident chairperson can distribute 3 x 5 cards, asking everyone to write down an opinion or an idea: "People are hesitant about giving negative feedback, so we'll do something different tonight. I want you to list two positive responses and two negative ones about the jazz worship experiment two weeks ago. Even about Bill Schlaughter's saxophone! We'll make this anonymous. I'll collect the cards and read them to get us started."

With such a procedure, even the quiet members will often enter a discussion to enlarge upon their own written comments. If they do not, they have still made their contribution. The hierarchical has been made more democratic. The church at large has actualized just that bit more its calling as the whole people of God.

Writing on 3 x 5 cards also helps long-winded people become more precise. It is one method of control for those who repeat themselves in spoken dialogue. The method should not be used in low-income rural or inner-city parishes where there may be members whose skills with written prose are limited enough to embarrass them.

Using Members' Gifts

The life of faith provides us perspective on the world. Perspective makes the difference between despair and hope. The same situation seems bleak to one person, fraught with possibilities to another. We need a positive perspective on the varied personalities and talent that people bring to meetings.

The key word in coping with the motley array of personalities in a group is *gift*. Instead of seeing only resistance or simplemindedness in people, the Christian sees gifts. That perspective implies gratitude for the other person, a search for God-given possibility, and a challenge to better, more faithful interaction.

Think of the various gifts and roles that members play in meetings.

The Expediter

The designated leader or chairperson may have to fill this role, but usually someone else can be counted on. Sarah Jenson is known as a "little nervous." She has a sharp tongue, born of her impatience. Group-life experts would call her "task-oriented." Sarah needs to trust God more and her own hope for self-justification less, but while that spiritual growth goes on, her drive toward less dillydallying and more task accomplishment can be gratefully received by a leader. Sarah is a gift.

One priest who was offering his parish a course in church history knew that his ulterior goal was for greater coherence and caring in a cold and intellectually haughty congregation. The format called for coffee and dessert. Daryl, the priest, consciously refrained from ever calling the group away from coffee to the topic at hand. He left it to chance—and it worked well—that someone else would come forward to say, "I think it's time for us to start." Meanwhile, Daryl involved himself in furthering new and deeper interpersonal pastoral concern among his flock.

The Silent Observer

Not all nonexpressive people are nonparticipants. They may be taciturn, reserved. The Finns tell a story on themselves. On their thirtieth wedding anniversary Elsa was seen by Olaf to have a tear running down her cheek. Olaf inquired as to the reason for Elsa's evident sadness. Elsa confessed, "Today's our thirtieth anniversary, and you haven't even told me that you love me." Olaf made his reply: "I told you thirty years ago I love you. I promise I'll tell you if I change my mind."

But Olaf may have other gifts. His very steadiness and patience may balance out someone else's impetuosity. He is not a nonparticipant. He attends more regularly than most members do. We may want to proceed by addressing specific questions to him: "Are we making progress, Olaf? Do you see any flaws in this new proposal?" Discerning Olaf's gifts is the key, circumventing one's frustration with his silence.

The Reconciler

Christians tell heroic stories about the saints who stood firm in the face of temptation. That noble posture can inspire something in us that is quite different from courage, however—intransigence. Meetings that work need reconcilers who can help others see the advantage in negotiated settlement.

We can take a cue from St. Paul himself, who was one of those saints. Paul says that Christ is God's way of reconciling the world to its divine ground and that thereby God makes us all ambassadors of reconciliation.

The reconciler does two things for us—one emotional, one conceptual. Both are important. Emotionally, the reconciler may have a gift of unusual sensitivity, discerning a group member's malaise almost before that person does. The reconciler then speaks up. "Patrick, you are unhappy with this argument, I think. Is someone getting run over? Do you feel that way?"

The intellectual aspect is a gift of other reconcilers. They help us see how two disparate ideas can actually mesh with each other. Sometimes this is the result of compromise, when two sides meet each other half way, as we say. The reconciler makes a suggestion that fosters a win-win result instead of win-lose.

Often, in church meetings, the reconciler calls back group discussion from secular language to the perspectives of faith. A financial committee has been fretting and fixing blame because the treasury's "balance forward" item had shrunk from one year to the next. Someone simply said, "This congregation isn't a business seeking profits. Maybe we should even have 'lost' *more* by giving it away. We're not in any financial jeopardy." In another committee, responsible for monitoring clergy ethics, a debate was considerably clarified when someone said, "We're not called to punish or even to fix blame in this case. Our main goal is to heal and strengthen the body of Christ."

The Process Observer

A rare gift, but one that can be intentionally developed in a group, is the process observer, a member who speaks up periodically to let the group know how well it is managing its task: "We're topic jumping, I think, and need to follow one line of discussion for a moment" or, "We should probably break up this issue into three separate questions."

The chairperson of a medium-sized meeting may want to appoint a competent person to assume this role, periodically requesting commentary on process. In larger formal meetings, a parliamentarian can be essential in clarifying process and ruling on procedural conflicts.

The Jokester, the Historian, the Norm-setter, the Innovator, the Encourager

We needn't pursue further roles in any detail. You may suggest your own. Some others that often emerge in extended meetings can be named. The jokester can bother people but, within limits, provides a light touch and can be appreciated for that gift. The historian or the old-timer can be a trial if the comments about how "it used to be" have a tone that also says, "and that's how it should still be, and it isn't." However, positively received, the historical perspective may be important and enlightening. "That's helpful, Dan. We never knew why teen-agers had that special role in the Christmas gift ceremony. We could keep them on and still include the fourth grade class I should think."

The norm-setting role usually falls to the chairperson, of course, but this leadership, too, is a function that others can fill. It may seem a negative, picayune complaint about meeting behavior that violates some standard. However, an appreciative approach can reap positive gain from this gift: "You're right. We did set an adjournment time at 9:30. We're almost out of time. Shall we table this and adjourn, or shall we by mutual consent, stop the clock for ten minutes to wrap up our decision, have one announcement, and then break up? Thanks for watching the clock, Sandra."

We will soon identify the innovators; every committee needs them, partly to balance the historian and the norm-setter types. And nothing makes the wheels turn more happily than the encourager, one who goes beyond gatekeeping to enthusiastic pastoral counsel and inspiration.

Generating New Ideas

New approaches to problems usually result spontaneously from our human curiosity and creativity. They come quite unprogrammed and unplanned. However, good meetings and energetic leaders can intentionally address the need for new ideas as well. Two designs for a meeting are especially helpful at points of frustration or times when new program opportunities crop up, such as the beginning of a new program year with newly constituted committee memberships.

Brainstorming

When a new year begins at St. John's, Bill Schlaughter asks for a half hour from the Consistory, and he leads a brainstorming session. He lays out the rules first: "This is a fast-moving, twenty-minute, right-brain, daydreaming exercise. There are no right and wrong answers. Every idea is accepted, no matter how far-fetched it seems. There is to be no discussion of any proposal. On the easel here the recorder is to put down something about each idea in a summary note or statement."

Then the pastor poses a question. One year it was, "How can we at St. John's attract the attention of the unchurched people in this town? Not convert them, not get them to worship; just get their attention. They need to know we're here." Another year it was, "How should we recognize the work that people do in their jobs? How can we help other people know about it, and how can we help people see their own work as a Christian calling?"

Bill uses the last ten minutes for a swift review of what's on the board or the newsprint, grouping similar ideas so far as possible into categories. Brainstorming on the question about making St. John's known to the community, for example, created notes under these headings: press coverage, art and religion programs, door-to-door publicity, children's programming, musical events, college relations, business relations, and civic clubs.

Brainstorming is enjoyable, sometimes hilarious. It often catches fire as a group plays one idea off another. The follow-up can be achieved by referring the records to a study committee, which is instructed to bring back specific proposals for further study, preferably in an order of priority as to feasibility or urgency.

Synectics

Another design for problem solving is less dramatic and more demanding. Some industries appoint synectics teams with diverse specialists to generate solutions to problems—an artist, a mechanical engineer, a biologist, a marketing person, and an accountant, for example. The theory of synectics is that cross-disciplinary comparisons invite innovative solutions. One synectics solution developed industrial storage economies patterned on beehive principles. Another improved paint-brush function with ideas from pump function concepts.

When a fairly specific problem arises, a committee may want to take time for a synectics interval. Perhaps there is a need to reorganize the church structure because of increased membership. Before revising a constitution, the congregation wants to review a wide horizon of possibilities. One subcommittee studies other denominational traditions. Another explores New Testament patterns of governance. (One scholar finds seven major types!) A third tries synectics—listing organic concepts from biology and plant or animal species. In fanciful but focused brainstorming they mix images—nervous system, octopus, eye and ear, dandelion, cell structure, photosynthesis, tree, circulatory system, lymphatic system, mollusk. The lively report they offer stresses information flow, program coordination, a more porous boundary for interaction with the community—all of which the Coordinating Council deems to be useful complements to the more orthodox findings of the other two study groups.

Or perhaps a congregation is building a new church. Before an architect is engaged, it needs a better self-understanding. A committee tries synectics to get its discussion moving. Members list in one column various kinds of *human communities*—club, hospital, convent, pioneer wagon train, army, asylum, neighborhood. Then they list images of the church from the New Testament. (A helpful academic book lists ninety-six such images!) They list bread, salt, leaven, body of Christ, wheat, people of God, lamp, city. And their reflection is under way.

Self-coaching

One of the most powerful strategies for drawing people in and for improving group function takes as little as five minutes at the end of a few meetings. The chairperson says, "Before we adjourn, I want us to look at our meeting as a whole and ask ourselves how we are doing as a committee. Did everyone get a chance to speak? Did we waste too much time or avoid the work we have to do? What do you think?" With that small review every meeting or two, committees almost inevitably train themselves to do better work.

CHAPTER 5

A Deeper Look at Group Process

Groups have lives of their own. Because of interpersonal connectedness, a group is not like a collection of billiard balls on a table. We can understand a group better by watching it as a whole than by trying to add up the separate actions of a committee's individuals. In a face-to-face setting, people's behaviors are deeply interactive.

Groups own histories. New aggregations of people—new committees—take time to become groups. Groups mature and then, like societies, need new sources of energy and insight to complement the wisdom of veteran members. Groups, like individuals, can enjoy themselves and thrive; they can get sick and die. They can use time effectively or squander it. They can even run away from their work. They have life stories all their own.

Learning the typical needs and behaviors of groups doesn't make group life wholly predictable. Human sciences are not like physics or electrical engineering. However, they do provide us solid information that can help in developing church meetings that work.

Four Group Needs

One way to assess group process is based on the question, "What does successful group life need?" Most coaching tools for group life will suggest three areas of need, the needs (1) for *cohesion,* (2) for efficiency and pride in *task performance,* and (3) for the *personal satisfaction* of individual members. I believe there is a separate, fourth need that we often neglect because we take it too much for granted: the need (4) for *vision.*

Cohesion

If a church choir is to do its job well, the sopranos need to listen to each other and also to the tenors, altos, and basses. Members needn't necessarily like each other as close friends, but they need to feel comfortable being together as a musical group. To build cohesion, choirs can interrupt their routine of rehearsals and worship leadership with a social party, a vocal jam session or an evening out at a concert. They seemingly turn aside from their purpose at such a time, but they are tending to a group need. Cohesion needs are often called "maintenance needs."

Newly elected, I once attended the first executive board meeting of a national professional association. I arrived concerned that we had only a single eight-hour day in which to do planning that could have used three times that. To my dismay, the new president, seemingly indifferent to constraints of time, invited us first of all to share with each other something about our lives and our work. The sharing took over an hour. As the day's intense discussions wore on, however, I realized the efficiency our trust-building opening exercises had facilitated. We worked as a team and drew on each other's resources far better than would otherwise have been possible. Cohesion is of first importance.

Task Performance

A committee meeting has a task. Most of this book is about achieving a meeting's purpose efficiently. The task may be selecting church school curriculum or personnel, or managing the church's buildings and grounds. Getting the task done would appear to be the most important group "need." Full steam enthusiasm for the task, however, makes for an impatient chairperson. If unacquainted with other group needs, such a person easily turns imperious. Group morale sags and with it the group's effectiveness.

Personal Satisfaction

Personal needs obviously play a part in group life. Some of them are simple. A person near a window may be in a draft and chilly. Someone may be weary, uncomfortable with the furniture, or unable to see the chairperson or some other members. Jane may have had an unresolved disagreement with Jerry over a family matter and still be fuming quietly about Jerry's stubborn ways. Someone may have a child who will be adversely affected by a pending decision.

Some personal needs are actually met by the lively process of the group that enjoys its work. Others are more private. Little as they may be able to do about many individual needs, sensitive group members and leaders will be alert to these personal issues and responsive to small cues about them. The chairperson may seek out an unhappy person at a coffee break, make an extra phone call, or give time during a meeting for individual needs: "Most of us know that Martin has been going through a rough time since his father died. Martin, how are you getting on by now?" Or "Harry, I am amazed that you even started the research on that question, given all you have had to cope with lately." Those questions are prompted by concern for both the person and the group.

Vision

As then president George Bush learned during the 1992 campaign, the "vision thing" is a terribly intangible dimension of our common life. Without it, however, meaning erodes, and our common life loses verve. Without vision, meetings become empty and shallow. They drift into lassitude or preoccupy themselves with trivial matters.

We are fortunate in the church that most members of our meetings rehearse—in their Sunday worship, if not in daily meditation—the ultimate vision of what we are up to as Christians. National holidays do that for the whole society. The opening prayer for a church meeting is another part of sustaining the vision. Scripture is brutally realistic about this, reminding us, as the old Common English Bible put it, if there is "no vision, the people perish" (Proverbs 29:18).

A custodian at a hospital, who had come to be a friend of one of the physicians, was heard to say, "Me and Dr. Jones, we are in the business of helping sick people get better." That custodian had caught a vision. Committee members need a similarly broad vision, given the limited and tedious assignments they often have.

Even in the midst of debate it can be appropriate for a chairperson or a member to interrupt and reinforce the vision: "We have been going at this for half an hour, and we're getting bogged down. I suggest we step back and ask what the overall goals of our action project are before we continue our discussion. Is it housing for a few families, is it a change in the mindset of our community about affordable and subsidized housing, or is it the provision of racially integrated experience in our white suburb? Is what we're doing mainly a symbol meant to change our church into a more mission-minded congregation and a better witness to the whole Gospel? We need to clarify our vision and our mandate, and then our meeting will go better, I'm sure."

Patterns of Decision Making

A good leader knows both the significance of making clear decisions and the advantage of having people motivated to support the decisions. Many a decision is only nominal. It is a nondecision in spite of what the minutes say. No one is ready to follow up the decision with energy and action.

For this reason it is important to examine various types of decision making, any one of which can be helpful under the right circumstances.

Self-authorized Decisions

Plenty of decisions are made by one person. No one protests, and the move is made. Someone gets up and opens a window or turns down a thermostat. We are on firmer ground, of course, if we check out the decision: "Does anyone mind if I turn down the heat a little?" "I'll bring cider and doughnuts for a brief break at mid-meeting if that's okay." "I'll call the public health officer to ask about the campsite."

Decisions by Default

The weakest and potentially most troublesome decisions by committees are the nondecisions, decisions by default. The chairperson, for example, thinks it a good idea to participate in Habitat for Humanity, wants to save some time, and reports that he or she will reply to the pertinent letter by saying, "Yes, the church will cooperate." No one objects, but members' opinions have not really been solicited. No real decision has been made. Having missed the stories in the papers, one or two members may not even know what Habitat is. Others have no intention of giving up a Saturday for this project as the letter asked. It has become a project of the chairperson, not of the group.

Tradition channels us into many decisions by default. The committee has always met monthly and has been lax about attendance, so the new group will do the same. The unexamined pattern might be improved by conscious decision: "I understand this group has met monthly for years, but we may want to change that." The leader should spell out the question, gathering argument and eventual agreement on plans for a committee's life, lest inappropriate decisions be made by default.

Consensus "Votes"

Most decisions by small meeting groups are made by consensus. With bodily gestures and facial expressions subtly supplementing the words, a group rapidly moves through many steps of planning and administration. Much of the process is subconscious. Agreed—that we speed up here; that we need a laugh; that we'll let Jackson speak up now; that we'll ignore Jackson; that in spite of the horseplay, we are actually moving toward firmer ground in this debate; that in spite of difficulties yet to be discussed, we'll probably end up cooperating with the Presbyterians on the soup kitchen. All of this might be spelled out in parliamentary fashion with motions on procedure and substance, counting and recording votes. Chances are, however, all that would be counterproductive. Outright voting, when there is a mild disagreement from a small minority, forces people to choose up sides unnecessarily. It slows the pace of action. In small meetings, formal procedure stifles creativity. Robert's rules are for larger meetings or for procedures that might be legally contested. A productive small meeting moves in a different style.

The dangers of this meeting process are obvious. Quiet people may not get to air their reservations. The chairperson may be wrong in assuming there is consensus when there isn't. "Railroading" is easier, with destructive repressed resentments cropping up only later. Consensus decision making demands regular gatekeeping by the chair.

The leader can do a lot to sustain integrity in the consensus process. Identify a position when it begins to emerge: "I think we're beginning to move toward saying yes to both the Education Committee and the music people's request for increased budget. Am I understanding the discussion right?" Or "We don't need a vote, but I judge you want more time and would like to table this item while we get on to more pressing business. Is that your feeling?"

The leader should always nail down a consensus "vote" just as she or he would in announcing a formally voted action under Robert's rules: "I take it then that we are saying yes to a 10 percent increase in Education and also in Music. Am I right? {*pause, checking the circle*} So be it."

Church meetings have special reasons for avoiding formal votes. Following Jesus, we care about people who are left out, the way a vote might seem to leave the "losers" out. The Society of Friends requires unanimity of approval in conducting business, giving any single objector a veto power. Put more positively, the group waits for everyone to be included in the choices, refusing to move until every person can say, "I approve." In a voluntary association like a church, it is urgent that we achieve near unanimity on decisions, not just 51 percent. The resistance of a large minority can cripple a voluntary organization. Even Robert's rules make special provision for a formal meeting to reverse itself. Anyone who voted *for* the winning proposition can move to reconsider if an otherwise legitimate vote uncovers an unhealthy amount of dissent. The project might then promptly be canceled for want of a healthier, stronger consensus.

Straw Votes

The straw vote can expedite the process toward consensus in midsize groups and formal meetings. It allows people to be noncommittal but think tentatively about a proposal. It is a quick way to find out what a group is thinking. It fosters democratic process by uncovering puzzlement or dissent that might not have surfaced. If overwhelmingly one way or another, it may become suddenly clear that no one objects, that there is in fact real enthusiasm, and that no more time is necessary for an official decision.

Records

The importance of recording notes or minutes of meetings goes beyond the legal requirements of corporate enterprise and the concerns of the Internal Revenue Service. Records provide a base for moving forward. They help us avoid going over previous work that people don't remember well. This kind of redundant and unnecessary discussion helped prompt Jane Swiggin's impatience with church meetings.

Recording secretaries have considerable power. Some decisions are ambiguous enough that a bias one way or the other is almost inevitable in the write-up. The minutes will reflect the secretary's interpretation. This power to influence, through the record, the group's ongoing life offers further explanation for the tradition of reading minutes as meetings begin. Even in informal groups where that formal reading is unnecessary, a leader should review past actions and bring a group up to date as a meeting begins.

The Subtle Insights of Wilfred Bion

Wilfred Bion, an English psychoanalyst, watched the dynamics of groups as he worked with mental patients. Bion reached conclusions about group phenomena that provide yet another perspective for us as meeting leaders. Here, we can but skim the surface of his rich psychoanalytic approach.[1]

Bion found two parallel aspects to a group. It is a "work group," tending to the task that is its designated purpose, and simultaneously, it is a "basic assumption group." Groups have a subconscious inarticulate fantasy life, he said. They behave as groups according to one of three "basic assumptions." They may shift as often as several times an hour from one assumption to another. These patterns are "Dependency," "Pairing," and "Fight-Flight."

The "Dependent" group passively waits for its leader not only to initiate questions but to decide the answer. Most new committees, even when they have in them strong-minded people, depend on a leader to guide them, to tell them what to do. Groups that are gathered for research into group life, if suddenly left without directive leadership, feel quite lost and abandoned. At first, their "basic assumption" persists, that someone will rescue them from being shipwrecked, so much at sea.

The "Pairing" group is more subtle. Bion occasionally found two of a group's members, often a man and a woman, engaged in more extended exchanges. The group's members watched expectantly as if the pair would bring forth an offspring, a Messiah, Bion said, who would solve all their problems.

The third kind of behavior, "Fight-Flight," is more familiar to most meeting watchers. Groups tend to get their collective energy up for bucking a leader or a recommendation, either with resistance or "flight" and avoidance.

By remembering these psychoanalytic hunches, we may deepen our own less sophisticated meeting watching. All of us have probably noticed at least the first kind of behavior. We see dependency most often in newly formed sets of people. Attempting to place an issue before a committee, a chairperson is met with silence. Eperienced leaders know the need on such occasions to let the silence lengthen until someone breaks the ice. The most tempting alternative, breaking the silence to answer one's own question, simply perpetuates the dependency, subverting or delaying the meeting's engagement with the task at hand.

Some dependency is always present in the world of organizations. Preoccupied with other responsibilities, few members invest the energy that is expected of a chairperson. However, it is the task of leaders to fight dependency of an exaggerated sort, dependency we could well call sick. When a corporate board of directors is co-opted by management and fails to represent the interests of the stock-holders, it is sick. When an "inefficient" democracy yields its vitality to the demagoguery and "efficiency" of a dictatorship, it is sick. So is a committee that allows its chairperson to make all its decisions for it, and the leader is misguided or weak who does not or cannot prevent that.

The pairing phenomenon is less obvious to most of us, but something like it occurs often enough. It is a kind of group dependency upon two or three people when the larger committee membership should be involved. Capitalizing on the hopefulness and the interest that characterize the pairing group, the leader can help others join in on the deliberations and should make the attempt.

Fight-Flight is sometimes easy to identify and interpret, sometimes very difficult. People come late; they miss meetings. When a difficult or painful issue is about to come up, the group veers off task. Conversations splinter, horseplay intrudes, or the meeting seems to linger unduly on its previous agenda item. Without realizing it, the meeting is fleeing its work, avoiding it. Being alert to this kind of unconscious procrastination in face of hard choices, the leader may want to observe, "We seem to keep getting off track tonight. Do you think we're running away from something on our agenda?" Groups can be surprisingly inventive in their unconscious efforts to avoid painful subjects or assignments.

Most of us can probably remember almost as well a fighting group, one that collectively resisted a leader's recommendation or a teacher's request for order. A committee will defend itself against a leader who for one reason or another invites opposition. The leader may be a subject of what therapists call "transference," subtly reminding at least some members of past resentments at parental authority or of imperious supervisors on the job. The group as a whole gangs up in resistance. Studying groups that convene without designated leaders, some researchers have noted a pattern of "patricide" or regicide, rebellion that wants to kill and tear down leadership when it first emerges. Sigmund Freud found such a pattern in religious mythology.

The psychoanalyst models one further stratagem that is helpful to us. In group therapy, the professional makes interpretations that may be useful to the group while it works for insight: "The group today seems hostile toward me as if I were a scolding parent." "The group seems to enjoy the hurtful combat between Dan and Sarah Marie—like spectators in the Colosseum watching gladiators. What is our gain from this?"

As meeting leaders we, too, can play an observer role: "That information was well presented." "The questions are particularly to the point tonight." "I have noticed something and I am puzzled. We seem to avoid the sexual dimension of this issue every time it comes near the surface." "We seem to be reluctant to bring in new information today, as if the plans were already set." "Almost everyone has had a say in this decision. That's good."

The literature about group process is now enormous. Most of it is technical sociological research. Useful training manuals for better group

membership are not so readily available, especially for church use.
Nonetheless, anyone who wants to probe the shapes and subtleties of
group process will not lack for resources. A few such resources are
listed below.

Additional Resources on Group Process

Anderson, Philip (sic) A. *Church Meetings That Matter* (New York:
Pilgrim Press, 1987). A reissue of an older useful discussion sensitive to
group process and church life.

Berkowitz, Leonard, ed. *Group Processes* (New York: Academic Press,
1978). Papers on practical issues such as problem solving, individual/
group connections, leadership, group effectivenesss.

Forsyth, Donelson R. *Introduction to Group Dynamics* (Monterey,
California: Brooks/Cole Publishing Company, 1983). A survey of
research since Kurt Lewin, the pioneer in the study of groups. Good
diagrams.

Gibbard, Graham, John J. Hartman, and Richard D. Mann, eds. *Analysis
of Groups* (San Francisco: Jossey-Bass, 1978). Selections contributing
to both theory and practice, from several traditions.

Knowles, Malcolm and Hulda Knowles. *Introduciton to Group Dynamics* (New York: Association Press, 1959). An early, brief, and practical
guide to useful insights from group process.

Miller, Robert F. *Running a Meeting That Works* (Hauppauge, New
York: Barrons Educational Series, 1991). May serve for comparison
with church meetings, this written to help people "succeed in the business world." Popular, a quick read in 85 pages.

Mills, Theodore M., with Stan Rosenberg, eds. *Readings on the Sociology of Small Groups* (Englewood Cliffs, New Jersey: Prentice-Hall,
1970). Selections on research and theory by sociologists (and others)
from Talcott Parsons and Karl Deutsch to Norman Brown and Philip
Slater.

Mills, Theodore M. *The Sociology of Small Groups.* (Englewood Cliffs, New Jersey: Prentice Hall, 1967). A tightly written volume, with bibliography that introduces a reader to the many sources of theory.

Reid, Clyde. *Groups Alive—Church Alive* (New York: Harper & Row, 1969). The effective use of small groups in the congregation.

Tennyson, Mack. *Making Committees Work* (Grand Rapids: Zondervan Publishing House, 1992). Thorough, short (125 pages), but quite helpful.

NOTES

1. For more see W. R. Bion, *Experience in Groups* (New York: Basic Books, 1959).

CHAPTER 6

The Larger Meeting

Thus far we have studied those typical church meetings where face-to-face relations are the norm. On such occasions from five to twenty participants are likely to meet, sitting in a circle for informal discussion. We turn now to conceptual tools that make much larger church meetings work.

Larger meetings vary. They may be lectures in an auditorium, with a managed discussion among thirty or more people. They may be congregational annual meetings of a hundred or more; they may be regional as church assemblies. Larger meetings present special challenges to leaders and to the democratic process in general. Some rules that are even counterproductive for small groups now necessarily come into play.

Meetings of forty people and those with five hundred would seem to have little in common except that neither fits into a living room or provides face-to-face intimacy for everyone. Nonetheless, some generalizations apply, as do many of the principles already noted for understanding small groups.

Consider then the kinds of things leaders of a regional church body—a diocese, presbytery, or conference—might have to consider as they design their annual meeting. They will guide the work of perhaps four hundred delegates coming for deliberative, legislative purposes.

This larger meeting takes more advance planning than a small group. It necessitates printed materials, audiovisual equipment, careful attention to meeting space and facilities, meticulous record keeping. It means ushers and tellers. It requires a good public address system with microphones throughout the assembly area and someone to manage them. It needs registrars and a credentialing process. Who is to vote,

who not? Who may have voice without vote? Who is to be recognized
as a matter of official and unofficial courtesy?

Larger meetings require a parliamentarian because *Robert's Rules
of Order* and bylaw rules have to be more carefully observed if the meeting process is not to bog down in confusion or procedural disagreement.

In membership, larger meetings call for representative processes if
democratic values are to obtain. The pure democracy to which some
denominations aspired in the past—letting every member who wanted to
come have voice and vote in a massed national assembly—has proved to
be *un*democratic. These assemblies have been dominated by the regional
sentiments of people living near the meeting place. The leaders, who
have necessarily dominated the mass meeting for efficiency's sake, have
left virtually no serious deliberative process in the meeting's schedule.
Replacing mass "democracy" with representative "republican" structures
provides a fairer, more proportionate voice for various constituents.

Deliberative democratic process, even for groups of fifty or a
hundred, requires careful meeting design. It means agenda planning for
debate, smaller subgrouping for assimilation of new information and for
reflection. It means intentional planning for the presentation of alternative proposals so that implications of one choice or another are clearer.
It may involve the appointment of a timekeeper and special rules so that
speakers for and against a proposal have something like equal opportunity for speaking up.

All of this is likely to make a prayerful person wonder whether any
space is left at larger meetings for the movement of the Spirit. Indeed in
the church's long and meaningful history, most renewal movements have
avoided the crowds and taken root instead in the intimacy of smaller
groups—the New Testament house church, Wesley's class meetings, our
contemporary basic Christian communities in Latin America. Most of
the larger meetings have been occasions of witness from leader to mass
audience. Yet Pentecost included the testimony not of Peter alone but of
"devout Jews from every nation under heaven" on a day when three
thousand were reported to have been blessed by the Spirit and added to
the church. The Vatican Council of 1962 included active discussions by
hundreds of the world's Roman bishops, cardinals, and lay theologians,
and it turned out to be a successful deliberative assembly with historic
significance. We need not despair of all ecclesiastical politics as if the
Spirit moved only in the parlors and classrooms of the local congregation.

The moderator of a larger church or of a region comprising many congregations has a heavy responsibility. Managing such a meeting responsibly requires a balance between strong authoritative leadership and sensitivity to democratic process. It is easy to railroad agenda items in a larger meeting, but the church of Jesus Christ cannot in good faith run roughshod over the attitiudes and gifts of the people in the pews.

The Rules of Order, Briefly

Henry Martin Robert, an Army engineer and general, published his first *Rules of Order* in 1876, adapting for "ordinary societies" an 1801 book on parliamentary procedures by Thomas Jefferson. In this country *Robert's Rules* has been an almost universal handbook for deliberative and legislative meetings ever since.

Derived from practices in Great Britain, parliamentary rules have a long history. Yet, there is nothing sacred about such rules of order. More important than their particular substance is the need for commonly ac-cepted practices that expedite the meeting that drags, or in which a clique or presiding official oppresses or ignores a legitimate portion of the membership.

Parliamentary procedure provides for the orderly consideration of business by a group. Proposals are succinctly encoded in motions that are then discussed in an open but disciplined manner and disposed of with affirmative vote, rejection, or referral of some sort. Like the rules of a game, parliamentary procedure defines fairness, providing both a stable atmosphere, which lessens fractious, emotional irrationality, and an op-portunity for minority participation. The participant can question even the presiding official with a Point of Order or of Personal Privilege, or can question that person's judgment with a division of the house or an appeal to the assembly.

Robert's rules are grounded in the realities of human disagreement. Unlike the Society of Friends, they do not wait for consensus, which is a wise and plausible goal for small groups. Neither, however, do they allow easy tyranny by a voting majority. They require a two-thirds vote for motions that cut off debate. At the same time, they acknowledge the advantages of broad consensus. Someone voting for a motion that is found to have passed by only a narrow margin can move to have the

motion reconsidered. This allows more discussion or a modified proposal, lest the original vote prove more divisive than necessary.

A good presiding official for a larger meeting is well advised to
learn the rules of order. An authoritative manner that stems from competence expedites the large meeting process and creates a minimum of
dissatisfaction.

High morale and a sense of goodwill are as important in large
groups as in small. The fairness of the moderator of a large meeting is
indispensable. The desire to facilitate the work of the collective body
must override any desire to push through one partisan proposal or another. Levity and lightheartedness also have their place, as does considerable patience with petulant or peevish people among the participants.

A Digression: Organizational Process

Any institution functions best when all four wheels of organizational
process are turning—innovation, planning, program, and evaluation.
The names are less important than the functions. Altogether they help
establish the content of the larger meeting.

Innovation often takes care of itself as a response to the disequilibrium or "troublemaking" referred to in chapter 3. As we said there, all
manner of elements contribute to change in the church's life. The Research and Development arm of industry makes for innovation more
formally and purposefully.

The second organizational wheel, *deliberative planning,* is the
central legislative or decisional function. In a church board, this may
involve gathering information, testing convictions and hunches about
innovative proposals, uncovering additional dimensions of a problem
that is forcing change, or brainstorming for imaginative possibilities beyond hackneyed, traditional solutions. It means weighing alternatives,
advantages and deficits, long-term implications, and organizational
purpose.

The deliberative process eventuates in *operations* or *program,*
carried out by staff and volunteers under some sort of executive coordination and guidance. In the church, for example, after long planning the
vacation school may finally begin its two-week run and close with a gala
program for parents and friends. A confirmation class takes a trip for the

study of church history or work in a clinic in Puerto Rico or Mexico.
Carpenters remodel the kitchen as the year-long fund-raising efforts
through the women's bazaar and half a dozen chicken dinners come to
fruition.

Probably the most neglected of the four processes in church affairs,
evaluation, is the monitoring and feedback function. Neglected as it may
be, this function ranks in importance with Quality Control requirements
in industry. Regularly, any organization should step back for a critical
look at itself. After an all-church retreat, the next meeting of the sponsoring group should include an agenda item such as "Retreat evaluation."
If it was an ad hoc committee, its work is not finished until it reviews the
retreat's weaknesses and strengths. Evaluation provides new input to the
planning process.

A diagram may help.

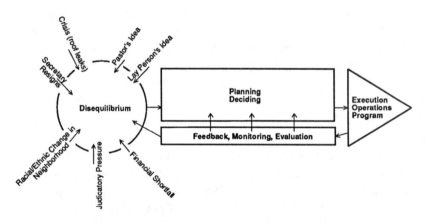

The Flow of Organizational Procress

(I) Disequilibrium. Some event or trend affects the organization
and prompts response. In a congregation, this may be someone's idea for
a study group, a neighborhood change, a sermon by the minister, a short-
fall in finances, a leak in the sanctuary roof, a publicity directive from
the judicatory, a forthcoming season of the liturgical year, the resignation
of a secretary.

(II) The response to Disequilibrium typically takes place in some deliberative committee or board in a Planning or Decisional Process. A regular or special meeting takes up the issue. Thereafter, (III) what has been planned is carried out. The roofer is hired, the announcements are placed in the newsletter, the teachers help their classes prepare for Advent, the interviews of secretarial candidates proceed.

(IV) Evaluation takes place in different ways. Someone approves the roofer's work and forward's a voucher to the treasurer. The newsletter readers react, hopefully, in occasional verbalized responses to the editor. The teaching staff, in cooperation with a board or commission of education, should be stepping back at timely intervals and assess the mission and operations of the church school. The personnel committee or pastor holds a periodic review of her work with the new secretary.

Note that the monitoring or evaluation may well provoke new disequilibrium that requires response, or, even more efficiently than that, may report directly for closure or further action by the Planning body.

This is an abstracted portrayal of organizational process that takes many forms as it is embodied. The schematic diagram offers, however, a helpful conceptual understanding of healthy and continuing process.

Bill Schlaughter and Rebecca Withers, the congregation's moderator under St. John's constitution, huddled an hour one bright December day to plan the forthcoming semiannual meeting scheduled for late January. It would be a meeting of over 130 people, for major decisions would be on the table. The Trustees and Personnel Committee were jointly bringing proposals for a second full-time pastor. The Missions Committee wanted to include cosponsorship of an AIDS ministry in metro center, and the Women's Service Club was proposing a task group for studying church memorial gardens. The fall stewardship campaign had come part way toward the estimated costs of the proposals. Consistory was putting them all in the congregational meeting's lap.

In his conversation with Rebecca, Bill began with a review of the four organizational elements above. They began, however, with Evaluation and Monitoring. By way of *monitoring*, Bill said he would urge each of the board and committee heads to do an evaluative and pulse-taking review of strengths and weaknesses in their arena of work. The report would be no longer than a single double-spaced page. Rebecca proposed that the reports be mailed out ten days before the meeting, and that each chairperson be allowed only to answer questions, not review what was already written all over again. She would stress brevity as she made contact with each chairperson.

The *innovation* wheel was already spinning fast enough, said Bill, as evidenced by the proposals coming to the floor. There was no need this year to develop any long-range planning proposals to give the January meeting some substance.

Both Bill and Rebecca thought the third wheel—day-by-day *program*—was turning smoothly, guided by Bill and Consistory, and energized by the positive feeling and devoted labors of scores and scores of active members. Both agreed, however, to read the evaluative reports carefully to make sure.

The fourth wheel of *decision making*, therefore, was the task before them, the January meeting. Rebecca was willing to allow half an hour but no more to reviewing the minutes and the evaluative reports. She said Consistory's motion to begin a search for a second minister would launch the deliberative part of the meeting. She talked to Bill about asking formally for an alternative report, something of a "minority report" from the Consistory members who felt a good staff of local part-time people could be assembled, at half the cost of the full-time proposal. Bill, although hesitant to confuse people with a second proposition, agreed: "Having that presented would give us a truer picture of our present feelings, and it will add depth to the meeting's work." Privately, Bill favored a full-time ordained colleague and a special funding drive to raise the rest of the cost. However, since he was able to live comfortably with either plan, he knew he also liked the idea of bringing in and trusting the congregation's collective judgment. He would make his own preference known only very mildly, and only if it was clear that it would not foreclose the deliberative process.

"Agreed then," said Rebecca. "After a treasurer's comment, and one from the stewardship campaign head, we will call for the alternative to be aired, and the floor will then be open."

Rebecca was ready to propose an agenda. She listed a time for each item, knowing that some flexibility would be necessary. She made parenthetical notes for her own benefit:

6:00 *Fellowship dinner*

7:30 *Prayers (Bill S: a hymn, a Lesson with comment, and prayer)*

7:45 *Minutes of the May meeting (printed in the advance mailing, no need to read aloud)*

7:50 *Reports received (all by one motion) and discussed*

8:10 *The Consistory proposal on staff expansion*

Treasurer's comments

Stewardship report

A "minority report"—An alternative pattern for staff at St. John's

Discussion (deliberative work, alternatively pro and con so long as there are hands up for each side, and then action of some sort)

9:10 *Missions proposal*

9:20 *Memorial Garden proposal*

9:30 *Adjournment, with benedictory prayer*

A very brief meeting evaluation form was to be left at each place, so participants could drop it in the St. John's "Feedback Box" as they left.

With theological conviction about participation and "priesthood" of all members in the body of Christ, and with large-meeting savvy, Rebecca and Bill structured a session that was both efficient and deliberative. Both of them wanted the congregation to do more than acquiesce in what some small group would dictate. Technically, Consistory could have done the work, but the scale of this change for St. John's warranted wider involvement by the people. Because Bill and Rebecca wanted growth in depth as well as institutional advance, they refused to manipulate the church meeting toward a preordained decision. Rebecca and other Consistory members with whom she talked privately anticipated that by 9:10 someone would move either to close debate or to have Consistory do more study.

The agenda would be published. Rebecca and Bill agreed that adjournment could be ten minutes delayed without a motion to extend the time, but that it would be better if not. It would be an interesting and useful meeting even if both the minor proposals were referred back to Consistory or tabled until the annual meeting in May. Privately, Rebecca hoped to give the Missions Committee a go-ahead on the AIDS project, with power to act, and permission for up to two special fund-raising projects. She also expected approval of the WSC proposal for wider study of their memorial garden suggestion.

One major danger in the larger meeting is passivity. The professor talks and talks while students mindlessly take notes. The long-winded would-be legislator drones on, and the audience begins to snooze. A wide and inclusive network of committee work is essential as an antidote, giving many members a stake in the larger deliberations. The U.S. House of Representatives with its 435 members could not function without its committee structure.

A question about "instructed delegates" often arises in this larger context. Should Sam Gross vote what our committee (our precinct, our state, our party) wants or what he thinks best? Members of a deliberative body are expected to *deliberate*. If they represent constituencies and committees, they have responsibility to report the views of those groups, but in the meeting proper, give-and-take is the rule. Sam must be free to weigh the issues—including constituents' wishes—and vote as he thinks best. Otherwise the body could be replaced by computers.

The chairperson of larger church meetings need not be a curmudgeon or a slave to rules. Rebecca was not intimidated by an agenda order she found in a rulebook. In extended daylong meetings, the moderator or planning team may schedule time out for caucuses or buzz groups. The chair may allow for some informality, some quips and stories to ease tension or tedium, a hymn to affirm the vision, a recess for maintenance and personal needs. *Robert's Rules* allows all these steps to arise from the "floor," of course, but sensitivity on the part of designated leaders is essential nonetheless.

CHAPTER 7

Meetings and the Pastor's Role

Half the people who read this book may be pastors or seminarians. They have some special concerns. Lay leaders of the church may eavesdrop or else skim this chapter.

I speak directly to ordained clergy serving the pastorate. You will hear many complaints about meetings, and you may resent meetings yourself. As I said in chapter 1, however, meetings are essential to ministry. Once you identify the value of meetings and use the skills of leadership, these sessions become opportunities for your work instead of burdens that stand in the way.

You do much of your work with people in their time off—evenings, weekends, late afternoons. If you have a family, you need to compensate for that so as to honor your marriage, which is a godly covenant parallel to that of ordination.

Three steps will help you cope with the problem presented by the way meetings can consume your time.

1. Evaluate your work schedule.

2. Reexamine your theology of ministry.

3. Develop new strategies for structure and time management.

Your Work Schedule

Remember that meetings are work time, not additions to an already full schedule of your "real work." Compensate for evening meeting time with daytime periods of leisure. You are on duty at a meeting, even in the informal chitchat times. You are alert to personal and spiritual needs as they crop up. You are perceived by those present as pastor the whole time. You are building the congregation's collective *esprit de corps.* All this means that when you choose to attend a meeting, you also choose whether to linger or to leave when the business is done.

The meeting ethos varies widely from rural to urban communities, from large to small churches, from one ethnic or denominational tradition to another, and among different pastoral personalities. A homemaker who hasn't been out all day may enjoy an extended evening, while a manager wants to get away for a night's rest before an early commute to work. You may linger with the homemaker or identify more with the manager. One of the requirements of pastoral work is the ability to stand up and depart when the time is right, to close off informal conversation appropriately. (One of my students, who planned to leave a parishioner's home right after lunch so he could study, reported that he "just couldn't get away" until 9:30 that evening!)

Ministry

As with other elements of our unique calling, knowing yourself is important. Check your motivations. Are you going to this meeting because you fear someone will judge you if you are absent? Have you forgotten the work of the Spirit and the gifts of the laity and think it all rests on your shoulders? Have you failed to understand deeply enough that Christ gives ministry to the whole people of God, that besides their ministry in their families and their work worlds, these people minister alongside you in church? (They *can* have good meetings without you!) Do you distrust people, so you can't afford to be absent?

By far most church meetings—subcommittees, teachers' groups, classes, and fellowship activities—do take place without the pastor's presence. A frenetic minister who tried to attend them all would not in most congregations have time for anything else. Dropping in on some, from time to time, is helpful, of course, if it can be managed. But the point is clear: We don't attend all meetings.

So which ones do we attend? In larger churches, the senior minister will rank as top priority the weekly staff meetings. In all churches, we will be forced to miss some less formal groups in favor of administrative boards and commissions. Even for some of these, however, a half-hour phone conversation before and following up on a meeting can replace two or three hours of meeting time in one of those busy weeks when every minute counts.

In missing an administrative meeting this way, the loss of face-to-face mixing and deliberative counsel is real, but there may also be some other gain besides the saving of time. The laity are given proof of their ministry alongside the ordained leader and priest.

If we conceive the congregation as a corporation and ourselves as CEOs, we will think we are accountable for everything. Then we grow compulsive about meetings. This directive model, however, is inappropriate. Christ gave his ministry to the whole church. We share ministry in a "parallel process."

In parallel process, each member, including the pastor, has a ministry, complete with small group meetings to attend. A diverse group of people are headed in the same direction. It takes some modesty, some faith in the Spirit's work, and some intelligence to realize that avoiding rather than attending meetings may be one way to foster the congregation's spiritual growth. Parallel process sees Christ, not the priest or the ordained minister or the lay leader, as the head of the congregation. All of us are servants, "leading," if we are so designated, so that the whole organism and its members may grow and "lead" in their own respective ways. We, like the entire church, are witnesses. Rather than CEO, the pastor becomes consultant to religious growth, counselor, resident theologian, and resource teacher/prophet.

New Strategies

Two practical options present themselves for implementing such a theology of parish life. One is to designate a church meeting night, a monthly time when all the major boards meet simultaneously. These meetings may be preceded by a fellowship meal and a time for study and/or worship. There may be a period when all meet together briefly for exchanging information before moving apart to their respective committee tasks. You as pastor will visit several of these meetings, but a lot of work has taken place in a single evening instead of consuming six or eight evenings of the month. And the collective mission of all members of the body has been strengthened by the visible church-work evening with so many side by side. The minister is out of the role of top-down executive leadership, no longer being the hidden, manipulative manager of every board. Moreover, this plan reduces slightly the number of available church meetings for that occasional lay person who spends too much time at church meetings, neglecting family or civic responsibilities in the Christian calling.

The other strategy makes meetings do extra duty as occasions of adult learning. They gather the congregation together through a common teaching missive for study during the first twenty minutes of the various meetings, month by month. The study document can be up to a page long but not more. It may be an interpretation of a Scripture text, an insight on the congregation's life, a "case" with an unresolved question at its end. These twenty minutes, which are usually concluded by prayer, set a meeting in context and serve the group's vision needs, as the older "devotionals" did. Chairpeople should note for reporting to the governing or planning body any specific suggestions for congregational life that arise in these discussions. In this way, these meeting starters can constitute congregation wide brainstorming.

Such an approach can make meeting more worthwhile in your pastoral eyes. It gives you leadership opportunity. The study pieces should relate meeting groups to the life of the church and should stimulate thought in others by virtue of their own thoughtfulness. Just as lectionary-scheduled Bible study unites Christians across a city, these help knit the whole congregation together because in any given month all committees have addressed themselves to the same question.

Here are two plausible topical discussion guides.

* * * * *

St. John's Church

Question of the Month

For use by all committee meetings during February

St. John's is moving from being one kind of a church to another, if the experts are right. I think it is our job to prove the experts wrong in one respect.

We are moving from being a "pastoral church" (150 to 350 members), they would say, to being a "program church." The implications are okay inasmuch as they mean we need to look at staff needs and may need to develop more small groups so that people know each other better and channel their learning and service efficiently. We don't want people to get lost as we grow. But if the experts say we are probably becoming a less friendly congregation, we need to prove them wrong.

For ten minutes, talk about ideas your group might have as to how St. John's might sustain our warm welcome for strangers and our sensitive caring for each other. Pray for that at St. John's. And have a good meeting.

* * * * *

* * * * *

St. John's Church

Question of the month

For use by all committee meetings during March

One of Jesus' parables may have implications for us these days. We used to call it the parable of the wheat and the tares. Jesus told about a farmer whose field hands asked him if they should pull up the weeds that had appeared among the wheat. The weeds didn't belong; they might crowd the wheat. But the farmer said, "Let them grow together until the harvest."

Here is what I'm thinking. Because we take pride in our church and because we're serious about how our faith shapes our daily living, we are likely to judge people of other lifestyles and of other faiths, even to the point of wanting to "pull them up." When we baptized a child recently, a single-parent child who had no father, someone asked if that was appropriate at St. John's. The deacons considered what baptism implied about our common life. They spent some time on this particular baptism's meaning for us as a congregation. They concluded that we were called to help this young mother raise her child in a Christian way.

For ten minutes, think together of ways your group and St. John's at large can be less judgmental, more helpful to the different kinds of people among us and around us.

* * * * *

Bill Schlaughter kept a list of texts and concerns for his committee study sheets. The next three on his list were these:

1. Galatians 3:28: That was Paul's experience. How can we make it more true of religious experience at St. John's?

2. Psalm 1: Blessed are those who delight "in the law of the Lord, and on his law...meditate day and night." How can St. John's be more of a "people of the book"?

3. Matthew 28:19: "Make disciples of all nations." We need to keep defining the mission in a religiously pluralistic age.

Bill saw these truncated discussions as an extension of the "Minister's Minute" greetings in the monthly newsletter at St. John's. They deepened the content of meetings, and they made up in a small way for a poor turnout at the primary adult education group, midweek Bible study. St. John's has no adult Sunday school class.

The Length of Meetings

We addressed this issue earlier, concerned for Jane Swiggin's complaints about church meetings. It is of utmost concern to you for much the same reason. If you choose to attend many meetings, expeditious meetings, cut to an hour or an hour and a half, will make your job far more viable. Again, differences like those between a rural and an urban ethos must be taken into account.

Many of the other suggestions in this book are meant for you, of course. You have the task of leadership development. You can function as a key gatekeeper since you may know people's reasons for reticence or imperiousness more than others. You can help create the mindset that expects meetings to be significant productive events instead of occasions of boredom and wasted time.

I hope you enjoy being a meeting watcher and love your people. Given that and some skills in group process, your ministry through meetings should prosper.

CHAPTER 8

Training Events for Committee People

With a little concentrated effort, congregations can develop the leaders they need. Basically, good meeting leadership involves two things: (1) sensitivity to group process and (2) the skills of leading. Some people come by both quite naturally. But others can learn them.

Effective meetings are so important that a church profits immeasurably from specific occasions of leadership development. These may be brief asides at routine meetings or more lengthy sessions when staff or outside experts share their gifts. Books like this one can help, but experience and practice in actual leadership are far better.

In this chapter I suggest a few brief exercises that will make for better meetings and then a more extensive daylong retreat with the same end in view.

Brief Encounters in Leadership

Making church meetings work better is as much a matter of attitude as of skill, but both grow stronger as we give them explicit attention. In the process the whole rich life of the household of faith will improve. Few things are more important, for example, than showing gratitude for jobs well done. The committee head who calls or writes appreciatively when a task is finished, or even while it is under way, contributes significantly to the meeting process. A pastor may find occasion to emphasize this with all the committee leaders in a church.

In such a phone call or note, a pastor can help others develop by pointing to particular skills and attitudes: "You did a good job of bringing out the best in those quieter committee members, Jane." "You

managed that debate well, from all reports, Sam. It sounds like you
didn't run away from the stress but kept tempers cool and ended up win-
win. I congratulate you." "I want to thank you for your comment last
night, Peg. You put the whole discussion in the right context, lifted our
spirits, and moved us ahead by a mile."

Calling a group's immediate attention to an occasion of good leadership is another contribution. In a congregational meeting, for example,
any one of the comments above would be appropriate.

We spoke earlier (chapter 4) of self-coaching at the end of meetings. A leader can also coach in the middle of a meeting. At the end of a
tense debate, Chairman Henry Perkins helps people relax but invites
comment as well: "That was a pretty heavy discussion we had just now.
I wasn't sure we had any tunnel's end ahead of us. Why do you think we
made it through so much more constructively than we did in that meeting
last April?" Or when a new program idea has been introduced without
immediate objection, Henry asks, as he remembers the four elements in
organizational process (chapter 6): (1) "What brainstorming will we
want to do now?" (2) "How much time will we need for planning?"
(3) "About when should this take place?" (4) "And how will we evaluate
this kind of thing to know whether we've succeeded and whether it's
worth doing again?"

There are other options. Most congregations have in them people
whose jobs involve skills in working with people and organizations.
Such people can be asked to sit in on a meeting and comment, or come
and share their insights sometime when the other agenda is short.

A Special Event

At a coffee hour Jane, Jerry, and Rebecca approached Bill Schlaughter
with a proposal for St. John's. Jane spoke first: "We've been sort of
serving as consultants for each other this year, and we want to make a
suggestion. Meetings in this church have been getting better. I'm beginning to see why Jerry likes meeting watching. What about a day
together with all our chairpeople learning how to make church meetings
work better? If you agree, we'll find people to serve coffee about 9 out
at the Retreat House. We'll arrange lunch and child care. Could you or
some professional meeting watcher types do the programming?"

Bill immediately said, "Not so fast!" But it took him only three more minutes of probing before he went on to add: "That's an idea whose time may have come. I will go with it on three conditions: One, that we consider combining it with an idea of mine—a long-range planning retreat. Two, that we open the retreat to all our members, not just the present chairpeople. And three, that we propose all this to Consistory and go through proper channels. If they concur, we'll be ahead. If not, there are other ways we can proceed—like making the retreat an effort of the Education Commission. This is a healthy, wide-open church. All this won't delay us long. And the process may give us more of a clue whether the combination of these two elements in one day away is a good idea or ill-conceived."

The Congregational Enrichment Eay

St. John's ended up with a day very much like the one Jane, Jerry, and Rebecca had proposed.

Bill and Jerry, along with two laypeople—Jim, who was in personnel work, and Petra, who was in college sociology—spent a half day planning content, while Jane's committee, with but one meeting and a lot of phone calls, took care of details—choosing a retreat center twenty miles up the road, coffee breaks and lunch, activities and teen-age leaders for children, promotion, and finances.

The retreat incorporated Bill's long-range planning concerns only to a limited degree. It included a brainstorming hour just at the end—focused on generating ideas for Consistory to use at its traditional planning session in May. Other than that, the design team decided there was more than they could manage on leadership development alone. Once into the work, all agreed they could have moved to a two-day format and kept usefully busy. They had discarded units of activity, for example, on the differences in how men and women usually communicate, on assertiveness training for women and better listening for men, on the Myers-Briggs Type Indicator, and on a three-way division among personality types that was a pet project of Petra's, "Scientist, Philosopher, and Peasant!"

They ended up with the following, as recorded in Bill Schlaughter's notes:

9:00 a.m.   ARRIVAL, with coffee and doughnuts

9:20   SESSION I, on Planning, Cohesion, and Mission at
            St. Johns

10:30   BREAK, more coffee, rolls, and conversation

11:00   SESSION II, on Group Needs

12:30   LUNCH & RECREATION

1:45   SESSION III, on Making Meetings Work

3:00   SESSION IV, Brainstorming Practice

3:45   INFORMAL WORSHIP

4:00   ADJOURNMENT

All the sessions were primarily hands-on and experiential. No lecture was over ten minutes long. All were well illustrated, and outlines were written on newsprint. In all, thirty adults were present, plus ten children. They made a large circle as they sidled into the conference room.

Session I

Introductions came first because St. John's growth meant no one knew everybody anymore. Besides a name, each person offered his or her denomination of origin and childhood hometown and one more item for a lighthearted touch: a number, from one to ten, as to the way the individual felt about church meetings, zero being awful, ten being great. Jane said, "Six," realizing that a year earlier she would have shouted, "Zero!" Lorry Powers, a speech and drama coach, then led a very brief theater game to loosen people up. She asked for people in pairs to mimic —as in a mirror—the motions, one of the other. After a minute or two, the partners shifted roles. Next, Bill Schlaughter spent a few minutes applying 1 Corinthians 12 to the ways a congregation functioned, arguing that different members—individuals *and* committees—make up the whole body. He used the image, too, to reassert Christ's headship of the body and his convictions about the nonhierarchical nature of the ideal church structure. Petra then spoke of her convictions that people worked harder and with much more satisfaction when they acted, without coercion, on their own initiative. She said she believed this sociological conclusion was congruent with Bill's convictions.

Next, Jim described a role-play situation and asked for volunteers. He got seven people to stage a meeting in the center of the room. The meeting, Jim said, was about the need for new paving on the church parking lot and the lack of any budgeted funds to do it. He carefully gave the participants new names and explained to the whole assembly the reasons for that step. He wanted to avoid stereotyping people later on during the day with roles they had tried on in the "parking lot meeting." He wanted the players to have freedom to experiment. Jim designated "Bob Buckleman" as chair, and the role play began.

Soon after the meeting began, Jim interrupted. Chairman Bob Buckleman, said Jim, was suddenly called out because of an emergency at his plant. The pastor had not come because he was out of town. Bob, the chairman, left the circle, telling the others to keep going; he hoped to be back in an hour.

Jim then let the seven member "committee" work their way out of the jolt of Bob's departure and stumble on into substantive discussion of the issue. He was able to give them fifteen minutes and still have twenty for discussion by the whole group.

During the discussion Jim managed to keep almost everyone consistent in the use of the assumed role-play names. About half of his prepared questions were discussed at least a little:

Which members were the leaders during the meeting?

What helped the meeting along?

(After defining gatekeeping) Who were gatekeepers, if any?

What would have helped the meeting go better?

What were the potential controversies?

Was there an adequate consideration of alternative solutions?

Were all the ideas presented taken seriously enough?

(Addressed to role-play actors)
How did you feel during the meeting?
(Bored? Let down? Impatient? Useful? Shut out?)

As he had planned Jim summarized on the newsprint during the last five minutes before the coffee break:

Leadership is a function, not a person.

Gatekeeping of various sorts helps people enter discussion.

Jim added a third point, however, because of what happened in the role play. During the review process, two St. John's people said the "committee" had been far too unimaginative about solutions to the parking lot problem. Jim described brainstorming and wrote:

Brainstorming can be very helpful.

Most of the coffee break seemed to be a continuing conversation about whether special capital fund drives to meet special needs were a good idea. (Some people insisted capital needs should be taken care of through the annual budget and stewardship drive.) Jerry used the time, however, to recruit players who would function in a role-play meeting of the Committee on Youth at Trinity-by-the-Seawall. The assignment requested each person to try to make at least one contribution during the "meeting" that fit in with one of the group member functions—expediter, idea provider, reconciler, jokester, and so on. Jerry enjoyed trying to match the assignment to what he already knew of the recruits.

Session II

As Jerry introduced the second "fishbowl" meeting at room center, he had Jane distribute assignment sheets to the outer circle, a score sheet for recording occasions during the role play when someone filled one or another of good leadership or member function. Each person was given three functions to watch for.

The Youth Committee of Trinity-by-the-Seawall, said Jerry, had a tradition of sponsoring a teen-age camp the week immediately after school was out. Its goals were partly to provide the occasion for meeting kids from other churches, who were specially invited, partly development of spiritual life, partly a time for three or four adults, always including Bill Schlaughter, to know the youth better. Attendance had fallen off in recent years, and it was not clear whether the church should continue. (Jerry had planted some ideas during coffee break—about opening it to younger kids, about changing it to a work camp on an Indian reservation or in Appalachia, the inner city or Mexico. He also mentioned a bicycle trip using the youth hostels, and the idea of a learning tour/pilgrimage to some historical shrines of the denomination.) The volunteer actors did not know what was on the score sheets being used in the outer circle.

The role play went well, many ideas and some arguments emerged, and Jerry had plenty of experiential material for his lecture on functions people play in good meetings. He took time to lay a little groundwork for the afternoon session by letting people reflect on their commonest contributions in a meeting.

Session III

Following lunch, Bill, Jerry, Jim, and Petra huddled to make sure the day was going smoothly. Meanwhile, others hiked with their children or with friends.

The afternoon focus was on conflict. Bill began by describing the church at Corinth and commenting that factionalism in that church was background for chapter 12 with its image of the body, and for the great hymn of selfless love, chapter 13. Petra invited people to remember and share with each other, in buzz groups, experiences in their histories when they had been in disagreements and to talk about ways they had resolved them if they had and whether they were still troubled if they hadn't.

Then she drew out from the whole circle material for two lists; one she called "Types of Disagreement" and the other, "Patterns of Resolution."

For the first, she ended up with these items: personal preference; money values; raising children; men and women things; politics; in-laws; religion.

The second list was shorter: Live and let live.

a. Finally forgave adversary; understood the other.

b. Argued it out.

c. Negotiated win-win.

d. Separated out personal feelings.

e. Used a friend to arbitrate, mediate.

f. Got professional help.

The buzz group feedback gave Petra plenty of firsthand material for her mini-lecture review of principles like those in chapter 3. She illustrated her points by having five members of the group—people she had coached during a brief meeting after church the previous Sunday—go through a mediation process. (Her situation was again from another fictitious congregation, this one urban, over whether to promise the fellowship hall every Tuesday noon for a year for a "floating soup kitchen" proposal from an interchurch coalition. Two in the role play were strongly for the sponsorship; two, also emotionally involved, were against it. Petra had to cut the debate off without resolution, but her teaching points had been illustrated well.

Session IV

For the final exercise of the day, Jerry introduced a brief set of rules for brainstorming, and he posed a real-life question he had worked out with

Bill Schlaughter: "In light of the present growth of St. John's as a family church, especially in light of *(a)* the declining number of whole two-parent families, and *(b)* the growth of cultural and ethnic pluralism around St. John's, what ideas should go into any long-range (ten-year) planning for the church?" The exercise proceeded with buzz-group and whole-group brainstorming and a final ten minutes for consolidating similar suggestions under about seven main rubrics.

The worship service included one singable hymn, a reading from Romans 12, some shared responses about the day's value, and prayers of gratitude for gifts and mission concern among the people of God.

Pastor Bill was pleased at the ground that had been covered. He admitted that the day on making meetings work had accomplished plenty, even without the three-year planning content he had dreamed of. He gave credit to Jane, Rebecca and Jerry, and to Jim and Petra, before he led the closing prayers.

The St. John's retreat was not the result of special genius. It was accomplished by dedicated leaders who planned carefully, who used resources well, and who had the kind of enthusiasm that inspired others to join in. Most congregations can do something similar for strengthening their life together.

Church meetings are special, since they gather in Christ's name, and Christ promises his presence. They are not the center of church life; worship is. But like the discussion on the road to Emmaus, as they build our corporate life they have an essential role in leading up to those holy moments of breaking bread and knowing Christ among us. I expect there will be at least a few church meetings—the kind that work—in heaven.

Welcome to the work of Alban Institute...
the leading publisher and congregational resource organization for clergy and laity today.

Your purchase of this book means you have an interest in the kinds of information, research, consulting, networking opportunities and educational seminars that Alban Institute produces and provides. Founded in 1974, we are a non-denominational, non-profit membership organization dedicated to providing practical and useful support to religious congregations and those who participate in and lead them.

Alban is acknowledged as a pioneer in learning and teaching on *Conflict Management *Faith and Money *Congregational Growth and Change *Leadership Development *Mission and Planning *Clergy Recruitment and Training *Clergy Support, Self-Care and Transition *Spirituality and Faith Development *Congregational Security.

Our membership is comprised of over 8,000 clergy, lay leaders, congregations and institutions who benefit from:

 ❖ 15% discount on hundreds of Alban books
 ❖ $50 per-course tuition discount on education seminars
 ❖ Subscription to *Congregations*, the Alban journal (a $30 value)
 ❖ Access to Alban research and (soon) the "Members-Only" archival section of our web site www.alban.org

For more information on Alban membership, books, consulting, and leadership enrichment seminars, visit our Web Site: www.alban.org or call 1-800-486-1318, ext.243.

The Alban Institute
Bethesda, MD